I0503858

Vinicius Rabello de Abreu Lima

Senior Equipment Engineer at Petrobras
Professor of manufacturing and assembly of API 620 Tanks at
Petrobras University
Former Professor of Technical design at SENAI – CETEC de Solda
Former director at VMH Information and Technology
Former Professor of Industrial Equipment at FBTS

Turning the Tide

1st edition

Vinicius Rabello de Abreu Lima

Copyright © 2019 by Vinicius Rabello de Abreu Lima
All rights reserved

ISBN:9781701273542
Imprint: Independently published

Turning the Tide

I dedicate this book to my grandchildren

Miguel Antonio

Rafael

Maria Teresa

Vinicius Rabello de Abreu Lima

Sumary

Turning the Tide

Vinicius Rabello de Abreu Lima

Introduction

This book seeks to bring to the reader a series of narratives created by the author, to share his experiences in the Supply Chain throughout his career.

In this book, all stories have been adapted to the present day, all reference about any company or people mentioned are mere fantasies and do not have any ties with people or real cases.

Vinicius Rabello de Abreu Lima

Turning the Tide

The supply areas of goods and services in companies, whether large or small, are often despised by the operational and production departments. Its technicians face daily the discomfort of, knowing its relevance so that the correct inputs are at the disposal of production, see their actions treated as ancillary, almost irrelevant, as if some product could leave the factory without the proper raw material and inputs being available in the appropriate time, specification and quality.

The theme is arid but vital to the manufacturing industry. Vinícius found a slight way to deal with this complex universe, its many concepts and its technical, administrative and human nuances, in a novelized text that puts the reader in contact with the fundamentals of supply management, based on examples and without being dull.

Vinícius goes in the essence of knowledge, in a history permeated with concepts related to the supply of goods and services that popping along the text of timeless approach. He achieved the feat of transmitting technical and administrative knowledge in a book that looks more like a conversation between friends, perhaps inspired by the nerds of Industry 4.0, which facilitate the understanding of things through "gamification".

In times of so many changes and mass contents, TURNING THE TIDE is a pleasant and consistent reading, for those who want to root concepts, usable always, without having to read a tedious compendium about the supply of goods and services.

Ronaldo Mascarenhas L Martins, MSc

Vinicius Rabello de Abreu Lima

Turning the Tide

The search for a new beginning

Sunday as usual, I picked up the family, wife and children, took the car and went to the beach in Ipanema. The path is the usual, Avenida Paulo de Frontin, Rebouças tunnel, Lagoa and Ipanema. The problem is to park the car, but I got lucky and got a spot on Praça Nossa Senhora da Paz at Barão da Torre street side.

On arrival, I step into my parents' house, already bringing the joy of grandchildren to see them, it is always a party. The eldest grandson, as usual, is the darling of the grandmother and the youngest of the aunts, Grandpa is equidistant, trying not to show preference for either one of the two, but it is difficult to hide the preference for the elder.

Our arrival brings a stir in my parents ' house, messing with the routine of an adult-only house.

My mother had just baked a cake, the famous cake of banana, the smell was amazing, just looking at it gave me water in the mouth. Nothing better than a coffee with cake in the morning. My father had just woken up and stretching himself in bed and my sisters still slept, because Sunday at 10:00h AM in the morning is early to wake up.

Gradually we were all sat together in the kitchen for a cup of coffee with cake and put the conversations in day. We were at the end of March, strong sunshine and the beach was inviting us.

The beach is the most democratic and economic leisure that you can have, just a bathing suit, a tent, a bottle of cashew juice, a biscuit and the fun is guaranteed. The kids were having fun in the sand and at the small plastic pool we brought in.

Gradually, friends begin to arrive and with them the volleyball game starts. Our group is from the old times, we have known each other since childhood and keep the friendship since then, having the beach volleyball game as a point of reference.

The conversation was amazing, goes from football, through politics and ending arguing about the performance of the beach volleyball players. It took all afternoon.

Late, my wife had taken the children to lunch at my parents ' house once, and the group is already starting to leave the beach, because tomorrow is Monday and it is working day.

We are almost in April and I was still unemployed for three months and it was difficult to get a job as an engineer in Rio de Janeiro at that time.

Although, I was relatively young with experiences in shipyards for recreational boats, maintenance of bulldozers, backhoe and earthmoving machinery, quality assurance for power boiler and pressure vessel construction and erection, but no vacancy. So, every day I got up early to search for jobs or an opportunity into the Rio de Janeiro industries.

At home, expense control was very close, but it is necessary to understand the behavior of the labor market. In this sense, my wife encourages me to continue to study, take specialization courses and try to add to my curriculum more qualifications, despite the cost of these courses, but we understand that studying is not an expense, is an investment.

We come home at night and I saw a voicemail on the answering machine. The message was left by a former colleague from my

Turning the Tide

previous job. He was asking if I would like to participate in a job interview in Campo Grande branch, which is about 50 km from my residence. This was a light that lights up.

The night from Sunday to Monday was difficult, the anxiety dominated the sleep, and when I realized, it was already Monday and as told by my colleague, I drove myself for the job interview in the first hour of the morning.

I had an old car, a Brasília/77 from Volkswagen, I filled it up with gasoline, checked the address and went towards the neighborhood of Campo Grande by Avenida Brasil. The distance was large, about 50 km and it took about 1 hour driving until arrival.

Upon arriving, I walked to the Reception Desk, introduced myself and waited for the interview. After 15 minutes or less I was called to get into CEO´s room. The CEO was a north American gentleman spoking a half-dragged Portuguese, introduced himself and asked if I felt comfortable in doing the interview in English and so I did the interview.

The interview was lasting more than an hour, when the Administrative and Financial director had joined us, so the talking lasted until lunchtime, finishing with the positive answer that I had got the job.

The next step was about all documents required by the Human Resources Department and a Labor Contract to be signed.

I had brought all documents with myself, that made things easier, so just after lunch I signed my Labor Contract. The beginning was immediate.

It was almost three o'clock in the afternoon when I took my Brasília/77 and drove back home. During the journey, while driving, my mind only had thoughts to thank my parents for the education

Vinicius Rabello de Abreu Lima

they could provide me, my wife for her support and encouragement to keep myself updated by doing specialization courses and the professional training skills that I have had.

Turning the Tide

The company

On my first day at work, I realized the challenge I had assumed.

I came from a totally different industry, focusing on pressure vessels and boilers manufacturing and shipbuilding and offshore steel structures for oil and gas exploitation, and now I was assuming a supplier development position in a new type of production industry, two distinct worlds.

The first week of work was intense, as I was linked to the Administrative-Financial director, we had meeting every morning with the board and with the Sales and Applications manager, which usually brought information about the sales orders, market share, competitors, customers and new engineering applications.

In those meetings, two main subjects predominated, the first one was about to the delivery time, which was always not accomplished by production, wearing the good relationship with our customers, said the sales manager and the second one was about costs. In accordance with numbers given by the controller, the contribution margin of the products sold was below the expected, it meant that the profit was less than expected, pointed out the Administrative-Financial director.

Not so often, they questioned about raw material´s price management, affirming that it was one of the main causes for a such less profitable numbers, causing a tremendous pressure at the purchasing department to reduce raw material's prices. I could see clearly now that I was hired to act as a COST REDUCER.

During the afternoon I usually scheduled meetings with those which were responsible for the other departments, because I needed to understand about the company's operation style.

HYDRO SPECIAL was a subsidiary of a foreign company, which had been installed in Brazil for just over three years and its specialty was pump manufacturing for the earthmoving machinery industry and implements, being considered one of the two best manufacturers in the market.

The company had two directorships, one responsible for the administrative and financial areas and the other one responsible for of production, engineering and maintenance areas. We had about 80 employees between direct and indirect labor, working in a single shift.

In sales department the team was very lean, there was a secretary, who was also worked a saleswoman, attended the clients by phone and the Field Engineer, who used to visit customers and others potential customers in a search for new applications and orders.

The diversity of products sold was very large and the quantity was not a problem, they accepted any orders from any kind and quantity, even from products that did not belong to the engineering standard, giving an idea of Taylor Made industry.

But despite of these problems, HYDRO SPECIAL was a number two in the market, just losing the first position to GENERAL PUMPS, another foreign company that held a prominent position in the market.

The production area was in a closed shed, with six meters high, without overhead crane and had three access gates inside. The

Turning the Tide

design of the distribution of the machinery was interesting, the tooling and maintenance sectors were in the center of the shed and the machinery for production were around them with a corridor of circulation between, as we can see at figure 1.

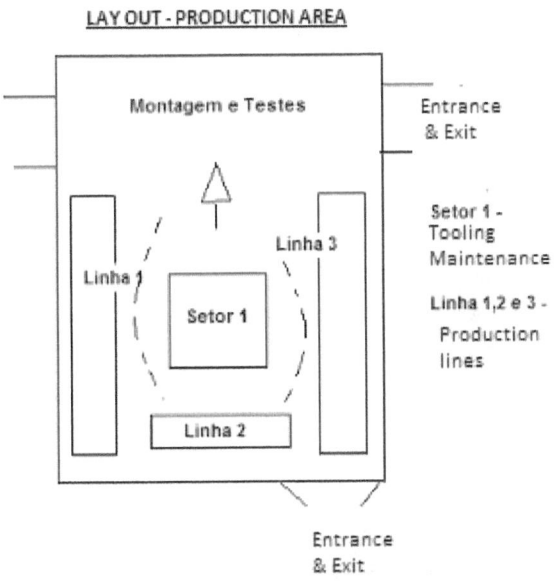

Figure 1-Manufacturing Area

The pumps were composed basically of castings, forgings, seals, bearings, fasteners, which at the end should be assembled and tested at the test bench and sent to the Warehouse to be delivered to customers.

The production line had as a main feature the high precision machining and this was done by just a few CNC or Computer Numerical Control machines and a large numbers of manual lathes, drilling, milling machines, which received the raw material that came from the warehouse into pallets carriage by a diesel forklift.

The production was controlled at the end of each manufacturing operation process through an employee, called Production Controller that belonged to the planning department.

The Quality Control department were in charge and had the responsibility to inspected everything. A single piece should be checked every time an operation process had ended. Everything was inspected by gauges and metrology instruments, through the inspectors of the quality control department.

The assembly line was in front of the test benches, and it was noted a huge quantity of pieces wrapped in wooden pallets and containers waiting to form a set to be assembled, giving an impression of disorganization.

The test area consisted of three test benches, two test benches for high pressure pumps and one bench for low pressure pumps.

The design of the pumps was provided by the headquarters in the USA, so the Engineering department had limited functions as it only kept all technical specifications and maintained all standards collection updated. They also translate drawings, specifications and adding some small changes when required by Sales or by the Field Engineer for new applications brought by them.

The development of new projects, when occurred, were originate in sales department and basically, consist of small changes into the original projects, generating new models exclusive to the Brazilian market.

The chief of the Planning department, Mr. Murtinho, an economist, over 45 years old, who led a team of three people, received me with a certain mistrust, responding to my questions in a monosyllabic way,

Turning the Tide

without any deep explanations about how do they plan or how the planning or PCP – Production Planning and Control as it was also known, was working.

The activities carried out by the PCP were such as manufacturing service orders, assembling service orders, and planning map for purchasing, were performed manually, all depended on the analysis of Mr. Murtinho.

All planning was based on the forecast and sales orders received from the sales department, generating a list of components to be bought by the purchasing department and another list to be manufactured by the production team, nothing very special.

Basically, the PCP requested raw materials from the warehouse, opened a service order of manufacturing, controlling them, follow-up its progress and when finished and approved by the Quality Control department, issued an assembling order.

The Purchasing department was commanded by a small Lady with painted hair in light brown color, always very well dressed, that should be about 40 years old, Mrs. Marta.

Basically, they received a list of what would be necessary to buy through Mr. Murtinho from PCP, made a search in a paper notebook that had the information about the major suppliers of goods and services. Thus, they selected suppliers and issued the purchase order, making this department very similar to a secretariat routine.

Since my arrival, the first point was in which room I would be allocated, because this is a new department had not been predicted. The solution proposed was to open a room at the Purchasing department, because Supplier Development department had affinities with the Supply Chain, so, I ended up having my working desk installed over there, near to the desk of Bete, the secretary.

The first week had already gone, the interviews that I did throughout the week, helped me to have an overview of the company's functioning, the profile of people, but it was necessary to present a working plan, that means, to design the activities of the new department and put them into practice, bringing the expected results.

Turning the Tide

My experience in the Supply Chain area was based on activities related to inspection and qualification of suppliers, acquired on my activities as a quality control manager for heavy steel construction industry my previous job.

The expectation of the company was enormous, the Supplier Development activity was brand new at HYDRO SPECIAL and I was directly linked to the administrative-financial director, this increased my responsibility.

The main staff, represented by the others department managers, to whom I had talked to, were excited about it and wishing that this new department could help the company to achieve better results.

The challenge was launched, the next step would be to define the acting model, the deliverables and how the results of this newly created department should be measured. The administrative director recommended me to develop a comparison study between raw material cost and sales price.

The guidance given was very important, it helped me to define what to do first. Thus, action taken was to analyze the acquisition costs raw materials and compare them to the average sales price, taking the leader pump in sales as reference, the pump 13PB13.

The first step was to determinate the total cost of acquiring raw materials , or Total Cost of Ownership (TCO), considering only not the price that was paid for the merchandise, but other variables such as, freight, time spent managing the purchase order placed, cost of handling and conservation.

So for this first task, I considered, in addition to the amounts paid and its taxes, costs related to the management of orders, i.e. its insurance, money cost and the transport, determining at first approach, the relationship between the total cost of raw material acquisition and average of sales price.

From this, it was possible to extract the percentage contribution of each item in the total cost of raw materials and obtain a list of all companies approved and qualified to supply each item that belong to the Bill of Material.

The result brought a value of $ 455,00 dollars for raw material acquisition cost, without computing costs related to order management. In the end, the percentage calculated achieved the following numbers: pieces in cast iron accounted for about 40%; bronze parts about 13%; Forged 17%; Bearings 10% and the remaining 20% were distributed between seals and fastening elements.

Now, I had enough elements to compare the total cost of raw material acquisition against the sale average, which at that time was $ 1,200.00 dollars, it means that the raw material accounted for 37.91% of the average selling price.

It is far beyond expected, and according to studies made by the financial area, it pushed the Break-Even Point to 1400 units marketed.

This information served as a case to be studied and from which, the supplier development department would initiate its proposition.

Turning the Tide

Supplier development

I was based at the Purchasing department, I was sat at the right of the room entrance, using a small desk and an extension telephone. The Purchasing department was to the right of the reception desk, almost to the end of the corridor, it was the penultimate room before the gateway to the inner courtyard.

I was requested from my director to prepare for the next three weeks, a task proposal for this new department, including a comparative analysis between the sales price and raw materials cost, focusing in the usage of new technologies that could be added to our manufacturing process.

The meetings that I have had with the other departments, allowed me to collect information that would contribute to my proposal, whose objective was to have a database of suppliers, whose technique and innovation Technology could to add value to our products.

Another important point highlighted by the Board was Conformity, whose basis was the legislation against corrupt acts. Thus, all suppliers, newer and the usual, would be aligned with the ethics and the Company's Compliance policy, and Environmental Sustainability.

The products sold by those suppliers were expected to provide HYDRO SPECIAL a lowest TCO (Total Cost of Ownership) and achieve the technical specified.

Thus, another point was to draw up the assignments and the insertion of the new department in the responsibility matrix of HYDRO SPECIAL.

In general, this new department were supposed to act proactively in the research of suppliers, that can provide goods and services with high quality and technical background, providing State of the Art solutions to HYDRO SPECIAL, resulting in a cost reduction.

Thus, a list of attributions for the discussion and approval by the board was presented:

- Act as a category manager;

- Map the evolution of the supplier market, in terms of technology and capacity;

- Map the evolution of raw material prices against macro-economic indexes;

- Develop technological levers, seeking for state-of-the-art in matters related to new materials and manufacturing processes that can be applied at HYDRO SPECIAL;

- Evaluate the technological and market trends that can enable the products of HYDRO SPECIAL;

- Map the relevance of HYDRO SPECIAL in relation to the supplier market;

- Make available suppliers that meet the company's goals;

Once defined those attributes, the Supplier Development department, flag the pump 13PB13, that represented more than 40% in total sales and was considered the number-one in sales.

Turning the Tide

So, for the first steps, a program called Suppliers Management Relationship or SMR was set. This program would be applied at all suppliers, from the actuals to the new ones. The directives of this program were based in incentive actions involving technical and commercial issues. This participative model would bring our suppliers closed to our products. We could show them where their products would be applied. It was expected to receive suggestions for improvements on our pumps.

The research for new suppliers brought in its bulge the increase of competitiveness, new technologies available in the market by the introduction of new materials and processes, always aiming to reduce costs.

This SMR program allowed to define how we would approach the market, if in short-term or long-term contracts or if we would made partnership with the supplier for its development or we would make a strategic partnership, as pointed out in Figure 2 below.

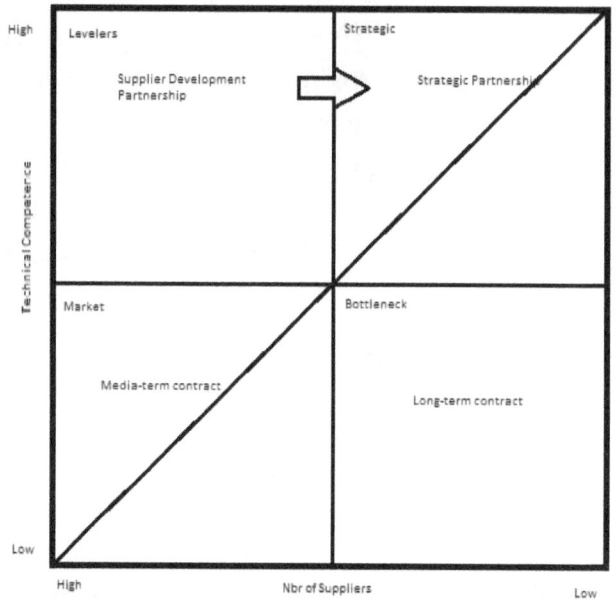

Figure 2-Supplier Relationship Management - SRM

However, it was necessary to know about the Technical Competence Degree from the market to achieve the requirements defined by the Engineering department applied at our pumps parts as castings, forgings and bearings, before a proposal of a procurement strategy to the purchasing department set place.

The Engineering and the Quality Control department together defined and established an audit criterion for approval of suppliers under the Supplier Qualifying Program, using the technical specification from HYDRO SPECIAL as a reference.

In addition to the criteria adopted by them, they were requiring the basic of the industry, such as, a quality management system certification issued by accredited companies by INMETRO –

Turning the Tide

INSTITUTO NACIONAL DE METROLOGIA and a proved manufacturing capacity.

The Quality Control adopted the American Petroleum Institute Standard, the API Q1 Standard, as a reference for the evaluation of the quality management system.

Silvestre, head of quality control, gave me the last results of quality management audits carried out at the time of hiring the current suppliers and some companies that applied for the time and have not been approved. In possession of this information, the Supplier Development department could understand the criteria adopted and determined the degree of technical competence from suppliers qualified by HYDRO SPECIAL, it was a very small fraction of the market.

The supplier's map presented by the procurement department only showed two GG-25 nodular cast iron foundry, just one bronze foundry, one forging, one bearing supplier and one heat treatment company, they were qualified and declared capable to provide as specified.

The information collected from the audit reports helped me to propose a procurement strategy to the purchasing department, based on the numbers of suppliers and the technical requirements.

As stated on the Supplier Relationship Management those two variables were enough to determine how HYDRO SPECIAL would look at market. We can determine that with a SMALL number of suppliers and with a HIGH technical issue and through the graph of Figure 2, it was possible to determine that the castings, forgings and bearings fit in the quadrant of strategic partnerships.

The next step is to determine which part or parts from our products would be economically relevant. It was necessary to know the stock value and how it was distributed.

Thus, it was suggested to carry out an quantity audit on all items in stock and in manufacturing, gathering their prices, their suppliers using PCP, purchasing and production labors all coordinated by an independent surveyor, sponsored by the Administration and Financial director.

The results of the audit showed that HYDRO SPECIAL had more than 3500 items registered in stock or more than $ 500,000 dollars and did not know which of them generate the largest expenditure. So, a raw material assortment took place, which means, all castings were put together using an internal material code, so as forgings, bearings and all others raw materials.

At the end we got all raw material items tabulated by model in a such manner that we could evaluate all expenditures versus quantities. These data put into a spreadsheet, resulting in a Pareto's diagram, as shown on Figure 3. This was a picture of 13PB13 model, the number one in sales.

Turning the Tide

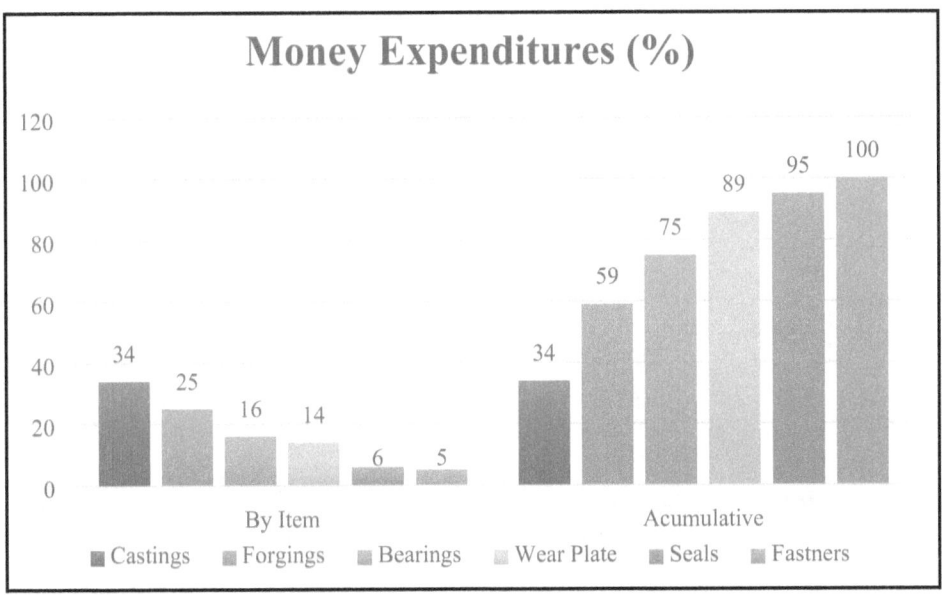

Figure 3-Pareto´s diagram for 13PB13 Pump parts

We used this Pareto´s diagram as a reference for the cost reduction proposal to be developed by the Supplier Development department. Based on this diagram all efforts should be concentrated in casting iron parts, at first.

The processing of the data collected, gave voice to the board about their feelings in relation to the main cause of raw materials expenditures, in accordance to them, we were paying too much for those items or planning without too much care.

The readings of Pareto´s diagram on figure 3, brought the information that only three items measure up to 75% of the money expenditure, namely, castings iron with 34%, forgings with 25% and bearings with 16%.

Thus, through this Pareto´s diagram a proposal for classifying suppliers according to the table below was made:

Vendor classification	Raw Material	Percentage
A	Castings, forgings and bearings	Up to 75% of the cost
B	Wear Plates and seals	Up to 15% of the cost
C	Bolts, nuts and other items	Up to 10% of the cost

This vendor list classification was an output from the Supplier Development department to the procurement department to update their vendor master record list.

This picture containing the indication that a strategic partnership for castings, forgings and bearings should be developed.

The propositions made by the Supplier Development team to the board and to all others department managers, such as procurement and planning, ratified its operationality as category manager for strategic items.

The Procurement department

The Procurement department had a very small infrastructure, all activities were performed manually, and no technology applied.

Therefore, as I was physically established there, I could observe from my desk, how a supplier record registration and the relationship between procurement personnel and vendors were performed.

In fact, the supplier's data were stored in a paper notebook form containing the company´s name, commercial activity, telephone, facsimile number, address, contact person and so many others informations required for registering.

Therefore, there was no mention about the supplier's classification and none about their performance indexes in attendance to purchasing orders deadlines, none about their quality, based on quality reports made by the Quality Control or the fulfillment of contractual conditions, they usually only asked for a lower price.

The procurement department usually negotiates with the supplier looking for discounts and better commercial terms. They were not used to propose a non-standard contract to them, which means that, their mind set were not used to propose partnership or even a long-term contract for the main raw material or maintenance items.

They did not have heard about Supplier Relationship Management methodology and how this could help them, so one of the consequences for not adopting this method were a constant claim for price´s readjustments, no trust on the lead time, an obligation to buy a minimum quantity, high transport cost, that in the end would affect our sales.

It was very common at the procurement department that the contract terms were established by the supplier as including pricing, delivery and so in many cases a minimum quantity order. The iron casting foundries were a good example, because, we had only two suppliers qualified.

We had the same problem about bearings or cooling oil for the milling machines, because we had only one supplier qualified for each item.

The suppliers usually did not have a single idea where their product would be applied and how important they were for the pump performance or at least, how their products were machined for example. There was no EARLIER ENGAGEMENT.

The procurement department was responsible for purchasing everything, starting from office stuffs to raw material for production, including milling tools, maintenance items for machine operations, computers and even items for investment.

Our main clients were planning and maintenance. Planning needed to meet the sales portfolio and the maintenance needed to keep the production machines running, so theirs demands were always considered a priority.

There was no protocol for receiving a demand from PCP or any other department, everything was almost informal. Generally, the demand was sent thru an internal communication form, describing what should be bought, quantity desired and time of delivered, no more data were provided. The procurement must perform the purchasing.

Turning the Tide

The demand that came thru an Internal Communication form, were processed in a speedy manner, focusing in prompt attempt, not delay the process or the receiving material.

The Procurement philosophy was that: "Material requested; Material supplied on time".

The department was proud to have no delay in placing purchase orders, all orders were placed in the shortest time possible.

Beth the secretary or Marta the manager, used to fulfill the purchasing requests received for each item manually. A very interesting point was how they selected suppliers. The selection process was based on their experience on the subjects, usually written in a notepad or through catalogues left by a commercial representative by the time of the visit, that occurred on every Wednesday. That was the selection supplier process.

Every day, Marta and Beth spent hours on the phone collecting prices, delivery and other conditions to issue a purchase order. Beth was a double-function employee, she was the department secretary and a buyer at the same time.

The routine for preparing the purchasing order to be signed was boring. At first, all orders were typed by the secretary, a black-hair medium-age lady around 35 years old, that usually arrived late almost every day. So, after typing, all orders should be signed by the manager and the financial director and this signature procedure usually occurred on the next day.

The procurement department personnel did not have time to discuss and think about how to optimize their activities, everything had just become a routine.

But it did not end here, by noon, when the secretary received all orders signed, she had to confirm those approved purchase order to all suppliers by fac-simile, teletype or by mail. These were the department basics routine.

All of these were done by just a few people and a very small infrastructure at the Procurement department.

The money amount involved in the purchasing of raw materials and in maintenance were significant and it was about $ 500,000 dollars per month, an expressive amount, in view of the company's revenues.

The procurement department had established all Wednesday as the day of the week to meet suppliers, from 09:00 AM to 04:00 PM.

They came from São Paulo, Minas Gerais, from the hinterland of Rio de Janeiro, and stayed at the reception room waiting until the time scheduled for the meeting. All of them were welcomed by Marta, in order of arrival.

However, only two suppliers did not fit this rule, one was Mr. Leonard from the foundry of nodular casted iron, a descendant of Germans, born in Santa Catarina, an owner of the Pouring Good Foundry, and the other one was an Italian descendant, a rude man, called Giulliano, from the forged supplier. They were considered the key suppliers for HYDRO SPECIAL.

The reason for this special treatment was obvious, the lack of any of the one these two raw materials would bring negative impacts on the company, however, in general, the relationship between the procurement department and the suppliers were cordial and friendly.

The transport or logistics area was also under the command of the procurement department. All contracts with carriers and transport service providers were under the direct responsibility of the manager of the department.

Turning the Tide

The service providers had two major responsibilities, the first one was to bring the gears machined to be heat treated and bring the ones that were already ready, because without these gears, the assembly line would stop and the second one was the delivery of all ready products to the carriers in order to forward them to our customers.

The activity in the procurement department was very intense and almost no time left to study and analyze the market, it was necessary to change.

Preparing for a Change

I was still based in the procurement department, I had a small table, an extension phone, which did not make direct calls, it was necessary to ask the receptionist to make the call for me.

In my daily activities, I was involved in technical specifications, drawings, specialized magazines and suppliers, focusing in cost reduction for the company.

It was June, Wednesday morning, I used to arrive before 07:30h AM, I parked my beige Brasilia/77, a Volkswagen car, as usual at the fourth spot on the right from the reception door and I drove myself to the entrance, when I realized that the board had already arrived, a white Chevrolet Monza was parked in the board spot, there was something going on.

The board was focused on achieving the financial and production results that HYDRO SPECIAL had been designed for and they were not measuring efforts to perform changes in the organization, whether by hiring new employees to occupy leadership positions, or by creating a new structure that would lead the company to achieve its goals.

In short, to meet the expectations it was necessary to change.

The process of changing that had begun in April, Marta, the manager of the procurement department, asked to be fired from the company,

Turning the Tide

because, her husband, an officer from the Army, had been transferred to a military base in Barbacena, Minas Gerais.

The board had been caught by surprise, nothing indicated Marta's exit.

On the afternoon of the same day I was called at board room and invited to take over the procurement department as well.

The responsibility increased and the opportunity was unique, company´s changing process was irreversible, it gave me an opportunity to assume a position at the Procurement department, but I needed to find someone to replace myself at Supplier Development department.

The opportunity arose with so many challenges. One was a new proposal for the procurement department focusing in Supplier Relationship management that together with the Supplier Development department in terms of knowledge of the market, and technical solutions would give to HYDRO SPECIAL a way to achieve its goals, by suppling all the company´s needs related to goods and services as expected.

A proposal was made based on performance of the procurement department, which passed through in changing work routines, add new functions and create a new structure.

The proposal brought to the department some new assignments that include the usage of technologies, as a computerized system.

We hired Mr. Antonio, an 18 years old programmer to develop a computer program to control all purchase orders. We had just a small budget for this kind of investment, so we bought a TRS-80 model computer with 48k of internal memory, two 180k floppy disk and small printer, this was our first Personal Computer.

Antonio had very good knowledge on COBOL programming and did the first software for the procurement department close to one month.

Beth was very happy, because from now one, she would not have to type the purchase order anymore. It was time to fulfill the supplier's database. We were proud about our small system, Antonio had done a great job, it was amazing.

Thus, another assignment was a Statistic & Planning sector specialized in macroeconomic indexes that would provide a cost evolution for raw materials classified as A and a procurement planning strategy, all supported by an in house developed software.

The new department had increased from three to five employees, manager include, and its final structure had been defined, according to the organization chart at Figure 4.

The change had to go on.

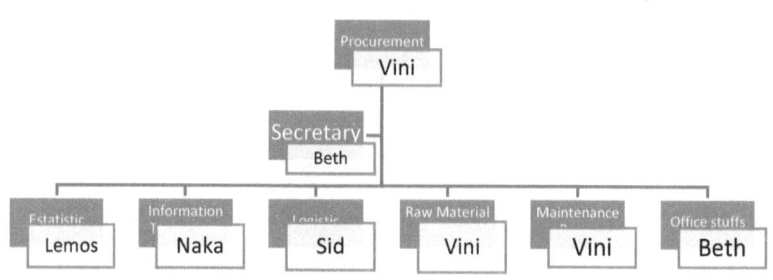

Figure 4-New Procurement Organization Chart

Turning the Tide

A new mind set was in a way and must be understood by all employees. We had proposed an interaction routine to exchange ours experiences to others departments, we want them to know that we were engaged into their problems.

We felt a necessity to stimulate and disseminate a program to accept new ideas, new procedures and to show how those actions could add value to the Procurement department's clients.

To achieve the values that we were looking for, we targeted to measure the quality of service provided by us, creating the sense of value from what had being done, spreading out all the results obtained, creating an environment of continuous improvement.

Two actions were soon implemented, the first one was to create and approved the usage of a form for all purchasing material request for any good or service for any other purpose.

The second one was the establishment of supplying terms for goods and services to HYDRO SPECIAL, that would be linked to the purchase order, which was forwarded to the supplier.

The new purchasing request should contain all the demand information and must be approved by the issuer manager, becoming the official document between all departments and the procurement.

The structure was updated, an area of Statistics and Planning was created with the responsibility to follow-up raw material's price into the national market, especially for castings and forgings, to prepare a briefing about the behavior of the Brazilian currency against the dollar and established an index about raw material cost versus cost of products sold.

We expected that, this new Statistic area would give us the opportunity to understand the behavior of those commodities against the Brazilian macroeconomic indexes.

Lemos was hired for the Statistic area, he was graduated recently in economy, and like everyone that was graduated recently, brought with himself the spirit of renovation from the Academy and, in a short time demonstrated a great knowledge about it.

We were performing macroeconomic indexes for the company, that would help us to measure our results.

The second point was the adoption of technology in the procurement process. The development and implementation of a MRP software, named SIVAE, was done in house by a group of young programmers. Pedro Nakayama led this group and he was recommended by Antonio Carlos, the former programmer.

Pedro was a COBOL, C+ and Clipper skilled programmer and led this task with a team of two young programmers, they had made a very good job.

I had gotten a budget approval of $10,000 dollars to buy new personal computers, IBM-PC compatible, one as a server, no-break, a 132 columns printer and software for programming development.

The SIVAE (Procurement system) were design to process all raw material needs to attempt sales. The SIVAE input were a sales forecast, a bill of material, standard machining time, supplier database and the inventory. The system output was the purchase order, inventory control, payment cash flow, in time delivery management, supplier performance, all integrated with PCP. The economic data were exported to the Statistic department to prepare macroeconomics indexes evolution.

The department team was complete. Beth was handling the secretariat and purchases of maintenance materials and office stuffs, I was in charge with all purchasing related to raw materials, Lemos in

Turning the Tide

charge of statistics and planning, Nakayama in information technology and Sidronilho in logistics.

And for supplier development a young engineer, Mr. Wiliam.

The next movement was in the department's operation system. It was imperative to change the way we were selecting vendors, we had to transform our suppliers in a part of the solution and not part of the problem and the way I thought was thru an Earlier Engagement solution. We needed to transform them into partners, so they would understand our needs and helped us in achieving our goals.

Suppliers are very important to any company, no matter what they supplied strategic or yellow-page materials.

The difference between them is set in which part of an industrial process they were involved. Thus, for the suppliers involved with the production directly were categorized into classes from A for raw material, class B for services related materials processing, class C for machining tools and class D for carrier companies, Labor outsourcing (cleaning, cafeteria, security, etc.), and Yellow Pages.

In the past, HYDRO SPECIAL had adopted two criteria for raw material suppliers. The first one consisted in a technical evaluation made by the Quality Control and Engineering department for castings and forged parts and the second one was based on the lowest price and the tradition of supply to other companies in the market.

Both criteria were not enough, because they did not consider the relationship management with suppliers. The first criterion did not bring the perception of critical or strategic items and because of this, a policy of an EARLIER ENGAGEMENT was not developed, which made impossible to develop a strategic partnership.

The second criterion only targeting the lowest price, could not exploit all the variables and levelers to achieve the lowest TOTAL COST OF OWNERSHIP.

However, it was necessary to say that this outdated methodology, which were not adding value to HYDRO SPECIAL, did not collapse the business of the company. In fact, HYDRO SPECIAL was feeling comfortable with that.

Thus, within the proposition of change, a strategic partnership involving suppliers for cast iron was developed, aiming to minimize costs in castings production, through a long-term contract plan by HYDRO SPECIAL and the commitment new techniques adopted by the foundry.

The strategic partnership was not applied to all items and not restricted to castings or forging parts, so the change, needed to pass through a comparison analysis between prices practiced for castings and forgings and the total cost of the raw material applied in a product.

Silvestre from Quality Control helped us a lot, because, through the contents of the reports made by them at time of receiving the incoming material, the inspection reports made during in production, gave all information needed to determine the quality level from each supplier of castings according to the quality control criteria.

From the numbers collected, the Statistic section presented a study on cast iron parts showing that cast iron parts had 34% of representativeness into raw material cost. This percentage index was a driving force that impelled a motivating action to search for a supplier solution.

Thus, once again, the contract strategy was forcibly passed through a development of new suppliers, or in developing new techniques

Turning the Tide

and processes together with the actual foundry aiming a cost reduction.

However, it would be necessary to review the market Analysis done in the past, updating those values considering the complexity of the current supplier market and the relevance of the purchase to be made up.

Figure 5-matrix of the complexity of the supplier market versus the relevance of the purchase

The first action was to define whether an item was critical or strategic, so for nodular iron casting, a market complexity matrix was used as shown in figure 5.

Using nodular iron casting as an example, we got the necessary information to define how complex the purchase was. The technical requirement for manufacturing was considered as HIGH complexity, based on a technical specification from Engineering and purchase relevance degree was also defined as HIGH, because, castings were considered one of the main parts of a pump. So, from the graphics shown on figure 5, we framed the castings as strategic.

Another point about casting, was its complexity, they were considered as HIGH and so the relevance from the purchasing point of view, that pointed out how important a marketing analysis should be done.

Now, we could say that we had developed a new criterion to evaluate the supplier´s record.

Meanwhile, to put into practice a new supplier´s classification that linked the degree of importance of what would be purchased and the complexity of the supplier´s market should be in accordance with the following parameters, as below:

1- Technical capacity to achieve the specified requirements;
2- Production capacity in tons per month;
3- The manufacturing infrastructure to attempt a quality assurance program;
4- Rejection index at time of raw material´s receipt or during machining;
5- Reliability in delivery on time the purchase order;
6- Commercial terms;
7- Logistic;

The parameters referring to raw material quality were attested by inspection reports prepared by our Quality Control and forwarded in copy to the Procurement and Supplier´s Development department, always endorsing to the cast production lot and the manufacturing service order.

Turning the Tide

Once the quality control issued a report to the procurement department, it had an incumbency to issue a report about the supplier's performance from that specific period, and this information would subsidize the review of supplier´s qualification procedure.

All marketing analysis demanded by the procurement department was addressed to Supplier Development department to perform it together with the other areas.

For the marketing analysis, was adopted as reference the bill of material from pump 13PB13, the leader in sales, which all castings parts should meet the engineering specification for nodular casting iron GG25.

The technical specifications were rigorous in relation to chemical composition, mechanical properties, especially hardness and other characteristics such as machinability and surface finishing.

To meet the mechanical properties, there was a requirement that only foundries with electrical furnaces were allowed. This restriction was used for achieving the finishing surface requirements and mitigate problems with gases bubbles inside the castings and to prevent a reduction in thickness at the internal walls of the molten material.

The specification also required a usage of a die casting technology that assured such finishing and defined at least three channels for eliminating gases during the pouring. Such a requirement from Engineering department did not allow the use of sand casting or neither the use of Cubilot furnaces, which restricted the market.

The castings weighed between 8 kgf and 10 kgf in average and the purchasing volume was about approximately 20 tons per month, which was also a limiting factor, because very few foundries were able to meet this volume per month.

The market research brought to us a picture of few foundries, in fact two foundries, which fit the specified technical requirements, due to the complexity of the foundry and the monthly volume to be produced.

So, this picture showed that castings in nodular cast iron GG-25 and its suppliers were framed as strategic one.

The analysis now reached cast parts in bronze and steel forged materials.

The bronze castings had a high cost, about $13.00 dollars and forgings manufactured in SAE 8620 steel, weighing about 4 kgf composed the main items of high cost and were part of a list of components to be monitored by the Supplier Development department.

The fastening screws, in turn, were specified in accordance with the ABNT standard and, therefore, they were items easily supplied by the industry, i.e., they are normally supplied by the industry of bolts and nuts. Thus, they were classified as non-critical as so their suppliers.

Among these tools for market analysis, the model conceived by Michael Porter in 1979 in his article "The five competitive forces that shape the strategy", was of great help.

The five forces of PORTER are thus defined:

1. Competition between competitors;
2. Threat of new entrant;
3. Bargaining power of customers;
4. Bargaining power of suppliers;
5. Threat of substitute products.

Turning the Tide

In this market analysis work done for HYDRO SPECIAL, we elaborated some questions for each topic and whose solution is in annex I of this book.

The result of the evaluation can be represented in chart form, as shown in the figure below.

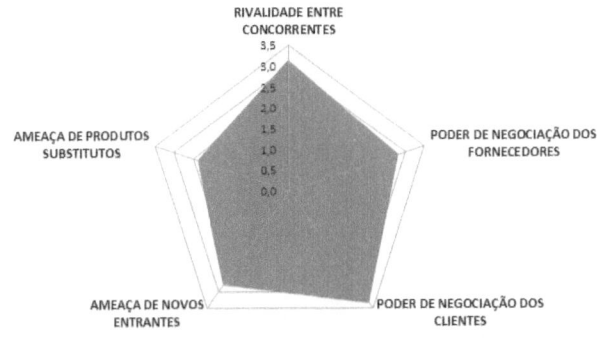

Figure 6-Graphic of the 5 Porter forces

The procurement sector began its modernization process with the implementation of a material replacement and planning system, a management of suppliers and a new sector for statistics and price monitoring, all of this, were in line with actual running changing process.

We have already developed a methodology and a policy with elements necessary for a supplier development program, supported by the Administrative-Financial Board.

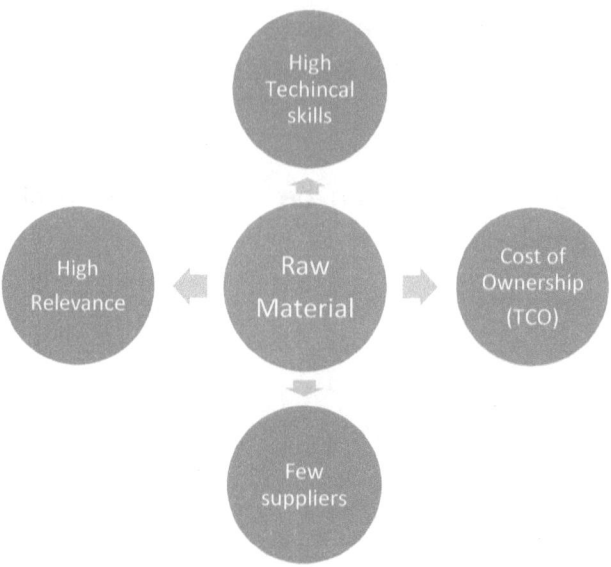

Figure 7-supplier development for castings

Thus, a systematic recognition of suppliers was implemented, highlighting those who attended and exceeded the expectations in quality, delivery time and commercial terms, through the issuance of a certificate of quality and attendance of HYDRO SPECIAL's expectations.

Turning the Tide

Planning and production costs

The pump 13PB13 was used as a case for studying and debugging all about the manufacturing process.

The Supplier Development was supposed to act as a category manager, that means, they did not only have to question about raw material cost, for new suppliers, but also to raise questions about our manufacturing process or from our supplier.

And the main question was: Could them do better? What should be done to enhance our manufacturing process and reduce or cost?

Thus, it was necessary to understand the market influences and the manufacturing process on our manufacturing cost.

At first we needed to define the cost composition, and we found that the cost was composed by MP ($) + CF ($) + INEF ($), where MP ($) is the raw material acquisition cost, CF ($) is the manufacturing cost and INEF ($) is the cost of process inefficiency, it is not idleness.

The cost of manufacturing CF ($) was directly influenced by the inefficiency of the plant, that means, by the fact that we do not convert all the available labor-hours into products sold.

This inefficiency was composed of two main variables, the first concerning the non-utilization of the total available labor-hours, due to the stoppage for bathroom, coffee break or even drink water, that was considered as a loss inherent to the company´s characteristics and estimated in 15% in accordance with the Controller, and considered that HYDRO SPECIAL was operating on its frontier of production possibilities as shown on figure 8.

This condition only occurs when we are producing at the lowest possible cost.

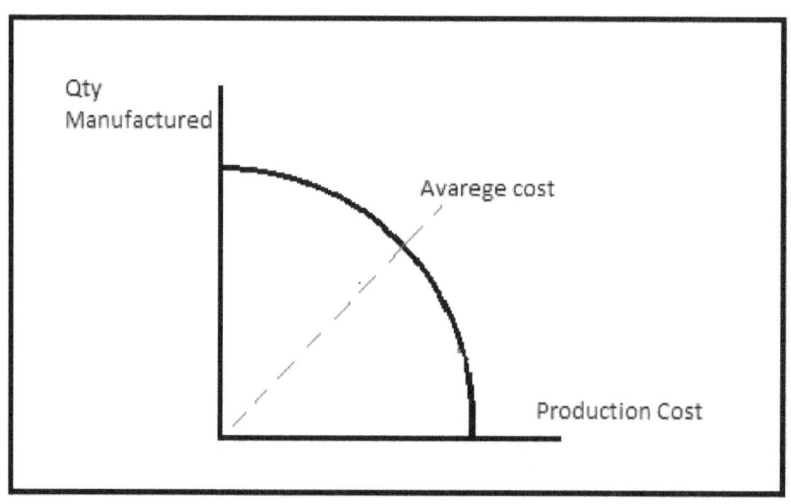

Figure 8-average production cost curve

The second variable was the manufacturing inefficiency, it was influenced by the excessive time spent in machine set up, caused by the usage of a non-automated tooling, by inadequate milling tools and lack of predictive maintenance, that caused a reduction in the labor-hour per machine availability. So, we realized that we should reduce the man-dependency on production, by investing in Computer Numeric Control or CNC machines and automated process.

Mr Ficher, an American engineer who lived in Brazil for more than 15 years and still spoke Portuguese with an American accent, was a head of production.

Turning the Tide

The production department had 35 employees working in a single shift and had Nilton as a foreman. Fischer, by his side, did not much care about what was going on, he put at Nilton´s hand all the responsibilities about the production, but the problem was that Nilton did not have much influence with the machine operators.

The engineering had a pattern for establishing or determining how many hours should be spent in manufacturing a pump part. According to them to manufacture a part or component, it should necessary just 0.58 labor-hours in average, assuming 85% as an index at the frontier of the Ideal Production Possibility (IPP).

Therefore, theoretical capacity to produce pumps should be estimated considering the following.

A pump consisted of 6 components or parts: one body; one cover; two wear plates; two gears. So, as we should work 220 hours per month, we got the theoretical capacity as follow:

IPP = (1-0,15) = 0,85
Number of workers = 35 @ 220 H/month
Total hours = 220 x 35 x 0.85 = 6,545 h/month
Time spent per component or part = 0.58 h
Number of components = 6
Theoretical Factory capacity = 6545/(6 x 0.58) = 1.880

This was the installed plant capacity in theory, so HYDRO SPECIAL could sell 1.880 units per month as a minimum.

The reality was different, the production could barely deliver 1200 units, pointed out to an efficiency of 63.83%, far away from the estimated 85%.

This discrepancy between the theoretical capacity and what had been delivered, created a huge backlog on sales.

The undelivered products had a strong impact on sales department and caused a wear between PCP and Sales and a huge discomfort to the Board.

Murtinho, was a head of PCP and responsible for planning the production, he usually sought justifications for non-delivery, as delay in casting supply, sometimes machines maintenance, or the excessive numbers of models to be manufacture, the point was that we were not delivering the volume sold on time. These justifications always promoted a warm discussion between procurement, engineering, maintenance, production departments with PCP.

The PCP had several attributions as receive the sales forecast, prepare a detailed list of parts to be bought and manufactured at the maximum efficiency, programming all milling machines using the parameters for production defined by engineering, track the production and for last issue the assembly orders.

We could not forget that the production capacity was defined in 1,880 units per month and not the actual numbers produced.

Murtinho was not used to be present at production site, he usually observed what was happening at production by a window close to his desk. From his room, he had a privileged view of the production area.

He felt satisfied when he noted that the production area was full of parts to be machined. The milling machines were fed in a frenetic come-and-go of containers coming out from the warehouse by a forklift.

The PCP issued a service order, it was a form that follows a lot of parts to be machined, according to the production steps.

In this form, we recorded the initial quantity, the scrap or tailings produced throughout the process and finishing with the final or ready

Turning the Tide

quantity, which would be forwarded to the warehouse or sent directly to the assembling line.

Fischer was always requesting from PCP few orders for manufacturing, but it should have a large quantity of parts to be machined.

He adopted the policy of "To do as much as you can" and as Murtinho did not like to go against Fischer, so all manufacturing service orders were prepared as requested by Fischer.

Fischer had a strong point of view about manufacturing, into his mind big production lots could absorb all inherent cost to machine set up, that he used to call as an economic production lot.

He believed that with large quantities the average cost should be lesser than with smaller lots, but in fact what we could measure was a big confusion of containers and parts spread all over the shop or production area.

This systematic policy of economic production lot adopted had given a false feeling that everything was all right, that our customers would be supplied on time and the company would achieve its economic and financial goals.

The production area was always full of containers with parts to be machined, there were a huge inventory of machined parts on production and at the assembling line.

We were facing problems at the assembling line, because some parts were missing, probably it was still in production. It was a mess.

Everybody worked hard, but the delivery of pumps to our customer was a disaster.

The sales department also helped in this mess. It was not unusual an interference in production by them, when they wanted to attempt a specific customer, in case of an event of delayed delivery, or to prepare a prototype for a new application. They were using production as laboratory.

Those sales interventions together with the idleness of PCP, regarding the policy adopted by Fischer in production, the inventory of parts in process had increased. I used to classify it as non-ready inventory in production.

The consequences of such interferences had affected the moral of machine operators badly. The constant change in manufacturing order, which one part was machined in detriment of what had been planned, caused a misgiving feeling whatsoever came from PCP, regarding to load machine programming. There were no more room to store so many parts at the production area, a chaos was created.

Another point was the increase of money expenditures due to replacement of raw materials. This extra expenditure had brought enormous consequences at our cashflow.

This production policy caused impact into several departments, such as accountability, procurement, controlling, finance and sales, but we could not forget the Board.

Elza oversaw the accountability and industrial costs department, was always nervous and stressed every end of the month or when it got closer, smoking a cigarette one after the other used to be her reaction.

In accordance to her statement, everybody had to work extra hours just because they could not get any information from PCP about production orders closed or still open. This lack of information gave her a headache because she must determine the Cost of Products Sold.

Turning the Tide

The PCP used to delay this information about the manufacturing and assembly service orders to her.

I did not know if this was true or not, what I did know was that PCP had not much control on production and so it took time to gather information about what had happened with the production orders. That was the truth.

It was not unusual to find production orders with more than one month in process, it was the result of production policy adopted by Fischer and interferences from sales department on production, so the consequence was the existence of a huge stock in production, which is not good. These actions increased production cost and capital expenditure.

This occurred due to an automatic resupply methodology based on the minimum stock with a resupply point and a production lot at maximum quantity as requested by Fischer, that turned into zero the castings and forgings at stock.

The PCP system immediately triggered a raw material procurement process for casting or forgings without any analysis of their effective need.

The problem was that we were only delivering about 1200 units from a forecasted sale of 1800 units, creating a backlog of 600 units per month and a problem between the Brazilian Board and the major company.

The backlog problem exposed a probability of cancelling sales orders placed by our customers, an increase in costs of products sold and a worse financial and economic revenues.

The economic and financial revenues from HYDRO SPECIAL was very different from what had been expected by the board.

The 63% plant efficiency had increased the Break-Even Point, as we were delivering 1200 units on average for a production capacity of 2000 units, that meant, it was necessary to sell more units to pay the same expense. This had to change.

Turning the Tide

The production activities started at 07:00h AM, then at 09:30h AM stopped for a 15 minutes coffee break to eat a sandwich with black coffee, and then returned to work until 12:00h AM. The lunch time was from 12:00h AM to 01:00h PM and once again a 15 minutes break for an afternoon snack at 03:30 PM and came back to work until 05:50h PM, from Monday to Friday.

The factory was splited into sections, we had the Lathe section, where the forgings were machined in mechanical lathes with manual chestnuts , this manual activity caused a physical wear on the lathe operator by the end of the day, and a consequence was a production decreased as measured by the PCP notes.

The Lathe Section had three lathes for roughing forged parts, a lathe with a profile copier, a gear milling machine and two grinding machines. It was the section with the best productivity according to PCP notes.

The other sections were composed by milling machines, which were a multiple head drilling, high precision milling and a radial drilling machine.

Those machines were operated by a team of 35 workers and all fed by a diesel forklift, which in a frenetic come-and-go movement carried parts from the warehouse to production and vice versa.

The adjustments in production left Nilton concerned, because it was quite often to stop production and redo the machine set up, due to a change in priority from PCP about what should be done. It was a mess.

The set up in a multiple head drilling machine could take over 40 minutes to change the tooling, for example. This usually happen due to a direct request from sales personnel to Fisher, the chief of production, who used to change the production planning without PCP knowledge or by decision from Monday morning meeting between Sales, Planning, Procurement and Board of directors.

This change in planning reflected badly in the staff morale, impacting directly on volume produced in a shift, decreasing the number of parts produced and made the machine operators spent more time in set up than producing. They knew that they would have to work extra hours to recover the time lost in set up.

The board anxiously expected for good numbers, making an enormous pressure on everyone, specifically at two department, PCP and Production. There was a common sense between the people from production, that Murtinho or Fischer will be fired soon, as noticed by coffee break conversations and supported by a betting exchange among the workers to know who would be fired first.

Fischer was fired by an unusual fact. It happened on a Thursday evening due to an occurrence of a soccer game into the production area, in the forklift traffic corridor, played by some operators from the radial drilling and the milling machine during the extraordinary shift.

The company had adopted an extraordinary shift starting from 06:30 PM to 10:30 PM to increase production and reduce sales backlog.

Thus, taking advantage of this episode of indiscipline occurred in production, the Board understood that it was time to make changes

Turning the Tide

in production, firing Fisher and some operators as a penalty and punishing the others.

The board made a quick move, they brought the Quality Control chief, Eng. Silvestre, to be the leader of production.

Silvestre had never worked as production leader but had enough experience in Quality Control and in serial production, a knowledge acquired by years of experience in an automotive industry in São Paulo, based on that experience the board made their choice.

Silvestre assumed production with two main goals. The first one was to recover the leadership from the production personnel and the second one was to increase production.

We were facing problems of low productivity due to several reasons, one of them was a lack of incentive and salary recognition, other points were about the quality of meals provided at lunch, transport and a new fringed benefit. These were the claim that came from production personnel and a headache to the Human Resources department.

We had hired a new manager for the Human Resources Department, Mr. Antônio Carlos, who was originally from the shipbuilding industry and had worked at the Blue Star Shipyard, on the other side of Guanabara Bay with the challenge of solving discipline problems in production and at the same time create an new environment that would stimulate productivity.

The time was running fast, we were almost in December and an initiative that came from Human Resources made all people happy. To celebrate the end of the year, they proposed a football tournament between employees and a party which included the arrival of Santa Claus.

The reaction was instantaneously, people get together to choose players for the teams for the soccer tournament and as usual, the most expected game, the game between the personnel from the office versus production.

The team from the office had employees from accounting, engineering and PCP and the team from production was represented by the milling machine operators and highlighted by Pinheiro the soccer game referee, a worker from Testing & Assembly who always protected the production team and the Office goalkeeper, Mr Paulo Renato, grabbing everything. He in his youth used to be a goalkeeper at Bariri Street team.

The families were anxious to see the arrival of Santa Claus, people were expecting his arrival by a pickup truck, but for general surprise, he arrived by helicopter, fantastic, great success. The Human Resources had made a touchdown point.

During the following weeks, all we heard was about the party, the soccer game, Production team victory by 3 to 0 and the arrival of Santa Claus, Antônio Carlos had just arrived and conquered the employees.

New year and old problems. Silvestre begun the year with a proposal to increase production and so requested some help from the procurement department. His first action was at the gear line, because all lathes are mechanical and they needed a technological upgrade, by replacement of all mechanical chuck by hydraulic one.

The machinery was good, but limited in technology, bottlenecking almost all lines in production. The non-upgrade lathes limited the manufacture of gears, making impossible to supply gears to the spare parts market and this was a constant complaint from our customers to the board.

Turning the Tide

The bronze wear plate was another issue, we were facing quality problems from parts produced by Bronze Brothers Foundry of North Miracema, a small town 6 hour-drive from Rio de Janeiro. And in addition to this quality problem, our machining process was taking more time the expected, turned it expensive.

It was not unusual to find casting failures on wear plates, increasing the scrap of machined raw material, that was, we scrapped the cost of raw material and the labor cost used during the machining process, it was very expensive indeed.

The wear plate subject was taken to Wiliam account, a young engineer from Development of Suppliers department to find a solution for quality problem that we were facing and to reduce the price that we were paying for those wear plates, if he could solve these problems, we could reduce losses and delays in the production of bronze wear plates. It would be a great challenge for William.

Meanwhile, sales department was still trying to keep its influence and interference in production, especially for development of prototypes, using our production line as a laboratory, using as an argument the production volume, that was too small and would not affect the numbers or the production flow.

Those interferences did not have echoed in Silvester administration. However, Murtinho, the guy from PCP, did not have intention to go against sales interference, despite of all planning.

This kind of action arose in all machine operators a discontentment feeling, that made Silvestre to halt this interference, in a once.

Silvestre was planning to improve production conditions starting from simple to complex actions, but in fact, he had a lot to do. Some actions were from quick implementation, others demanded resources and time, but all were necessary and had to be done.

At the Assembly and Testing line, Silvestre fired all and stablished the skills for team member, which were proactiveness and organization. A new team was set with people coming from other department and by hiring new employees.

We were in July and the production volume remained the same, that was, too much effort and little result. The last week from June was terrible, we closed June with only 1064 units delivered, justified by problems occurred with electric power supply due to a fire in the power supply house, caused by fuse box, that left the hole facility with no power for almost two days. We contracted a diesel power supply while our maintenance was working on that. We did not have any production emergency plan for that.

The July had come, and production was still going to the same way, despite Silvestre's efforts.

We were a week from the end of July, the subject for the meeting with the Board was the July´s production number, namely how many units would be delivered.

Usually the last week of the month was considered the best in numbers, the production always increased, due to some old production orders ending that lead more pumps to be assembled than for any efficiency process.

Murtinho had said that the number would be slightly better, about 1250 units and based in production history and his experience, that number was the real production capacity and not the two thousand units as per the feasibility study advocated by specialist from major company in USA.

The discussion was heated up among all, each one advocating a point of view, without a proposed solution. Murtinho was still saying that 1250 units were the maximum that could be produced with those

Turning the Tide

machines, Frederico from sales claimed to have potential for 1800 units per month or more since they could be delivered, so ended the meeting.

Meeting ended, Silvestre, Frederico and me went out for lunch, by the time we returned, we got the news that Murtinho was fired.

The supply chain

The procurement department, after the new organization chart, kept a lean structure with a very consistent deliverable.

The market knowledge pointed out our position on the rank on the supply chain market, specially into iron castings and forgings, an essential raw material for us and that we usually bought.

Another point about the market knowledge was the performance and commercial policy, including prices evolution. Those tasks belonged to the work developed by Lemos, who was using statistics knowledge with good results.

All of these, put the procurement department in another level, working in a high-level efficiency environment.

We had just started to use the concept of CUSTOMER-CLIENT relationship between departments, focusing in a better administration for all services provided by us to other department.

We started to treat all departments as a costumer and considered ourselves as a solution provider.

The usage of computers brought to all buyers an opportunity to access supplier's database directly from computer screen or from a report, searching for companies that could provide such good or service to us and then made a link to a request for quotation, which could be sent by several media, Teletype, Fac-simile or telephone.

Turning the Tide

Suppliers usually reply for a request for quotation (RFQ) in no more than one week, and as theirs RFQ answers were attached to a purchasing request, it was easy and quick to check and analyze their proposal and define the winner. Once the supplier was approved a Purchasing Order would be printed, signed and sent to them. The next steps were to do a follow-up.

William from Supplier Development had been done a very good job, he had developed another heat treatment company for gears and shafts, this action was a request that came from the Procurement Department and from now on, we would have two suppliers for heat treatment instead of one.

These two departments were so tuned that, it was not unusual for a buyer to request for development assistance when he was experiencing technical difficulties in the supply chain business.

The development of a new bronze foundry for wear plates, showed how tuned Procurement Department was.

A company named Bronze-Italia Foundry had been developed in order to replace Galo Bronze Foundry, whose quality and cost were the worst as possible. The Bronze-Italia Foundry was recognized by the market as a benchmark in bronze castings and had high quality standards. They had a high-tech pouring process, that in short words, all castings were done by centrifugation process of the melted material and then pouring in shell molding, producing parts with no porosity and with excellent finishing.

The high-quality parts supplied impacted positively, resulting in no rejection during the machining process and as their thickness was very close to the final and desired thickness, we would spend less time for producing wear plates, increasing the number of wear plates produced.

This new supplier met the quality requested by Silvestre and cost required by Procurement, in accordance with the new mind set, so the first long-term contract was established, that would guarantee a minimum monthly consumption and scheduled deliveries, this contract should be adjusted every 60 days and another point, depending on the volume, it was possible to obtain a reduction in unit price and freight.

The contract with Bronze-Italia was the first using the concept of JUST-IN-TIME.

The Procurement department had implemented new routines and process, brought alternatives to the supply chain, but still needed more accurate information about the demands from sales department.

We were back from lunch, the people from sales, engineering, and me, as soon my car passed the entrance, driving towards the parking lot, the receptionist came to me and said that the Director wanted me in his room.

As soon I got into his room, he told me that he had fired the PCP chief and would like to invite me to assume the PCP as well. I was surprised about that. We talked a little, he spoke about the bonus and the onus that this opportunity would offer and in case of acceptance, there would be no return point.

We were at the end of July, the production delivered 1256 units, as predicted by Murtinho. The given challenge came together with a message, that I had to reach a high production volume, or otherwise I would be fire too. I accepted the challenge.

The procurement department was working as planned and now I needed to find someone to replace myself in a hurry. This day I worked until 10:00 PM preparing a proposal to the board.

Turning the Tide

A proposal of a new department named MATERIALS MANAGEMENT made to the board put together PCP, Procurement, Warehouse, Logistics and Information Technology, after the meeting I got a approval from the board for the new department.

The Supplier Development department still be at the administrative-financial board hands.

I had to work hard to put into practice all that I had design for this new department. I began from the Procurement department where Lemos, had enough experience due to his participation in all raw materials purchasing processes as so the knowledge of all routines and structure cost as well.

The next step was to tell Nakayama that he would be in charge for Information Technology Department at the same time I had given him a task, which was to develop a planning software, based on MRP – Material, Replace and Planning to put into action before August, looking forward the goals planned. At last, I had to prepare the new PCP team.

The starting point was the production simulation using an advanced features of an electronic spreadsheet software, using as a reference the production times for each production phase in accordance with Engineering standards.

This spreadsheet gave us a tool for predicting what could happen in production line based on our mix of sales, so we could simulate the best production mix.

Another important action was the MRP software development. We had already developed a system for purchasing and now we needed to extend this system to all departments as sales, planning, purchasing, engineering, warehouse, so we create a MRP system, named SIVAE, which was in charge of the Nakayama´s team.

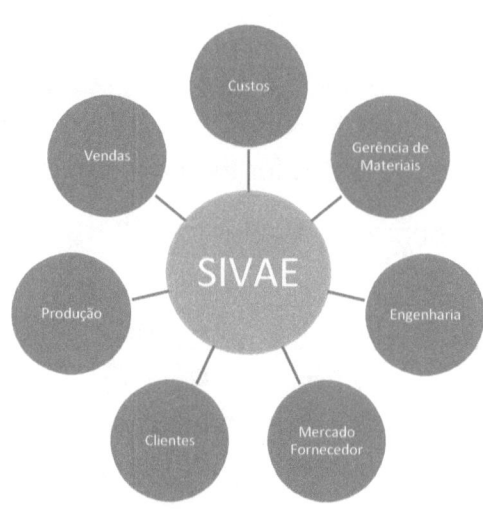

Figure 9-Sivae-Context diagram

The SIVAE used in its database as an input the list of components applied to all pumps with quantities and material specification, the standard production time from Engineering, data necessary for planning purpose. The system also used the sales forecast as an input, that together with the inventory and the incoming material, defined the planning for the month, that at the end the delivery time.

These informations were fundamental for production and purchases planning.

At the same time, the arrival of Silvestre as ahead of production, allowed us to start a discussion about alternatives and different ways in conducting the production line. These discussions were fruitful, because the difficulties on production would reflect negatively on the planning, that means, would affect the expected results.

We needed to find an optimal point between production, purchasing, planning and sales.

Turning the Tide

The bottlenecks in the production were known. We had limitations in the gear machining section, roughing mill and milling machine with computerized numerical control or CNC.

On the other hand, it was necessary to have more confidence in the inventory information as so about what was being produced, that is, what parts were in progress at production and the arrival of the raw materials purchased. All these informations had to be precise for the planning success.

The warehouse inventory and inventory of parts in progress at production were a fundamental action that had to be carried out. Thus, I called the warehouse foreman and someone from PCP, that together with a staff that Silvestre had put at our disposal, to do the inventory in production in half-day.

Nakamura, by his turn, had left his team ready for processing all informations that would come from the inventory personnel and issued an updated report about raw material stock.

The production was not stopped completely while we were in an inventory process, because we had a plan to follow. So, to do that, we had to permit that a part could be machined while the inventory was running, but it could not be moved forward.

This gave us an opportunity to make an inventory and produce at the same time, keeping our planning of manufacturing and delivering the predicted volume of products.

The planning proposal for production was, at the first moment, to return to the warehouse all parts that had not yet being manufactured and based on production inventory of parts in progress against sales forecast, we sent back to the warehouse every part that were not in the sales forecast or exceeded the sales forecast.

We did it with the help from an officer from PCP, from the Assembling Line and a Milling Foreman.

Nakayama had processed all inventory data and prepared a report sorted by part number, listing all parts in stock, quantity, unit cost, monthly consumption and the unit cost was calculated according to the accounting department guidelines.

This report had the newest data from stock and was distributed to the board of Directors and to all departments that might need it.

As soon as I got it, I called the PCP, Procurement and Warehouse foreman to check those data against sales forecast. This analysis was critical for production and an assembling plan.

Based on sales forecast, Nakayama ran a comparison list between parts in stock and in process against those needed at the assembling line, resulting in a balance report of what were needed to be manufactured or assembled. Thru this balance report we could schedule an assembling program and finally attempt the sales forecast.

This balance report also showed us the date schedule for the incoming material from our suppliers. So, in this way, we could prepare a production plan and a delivery schedule for the products sold.

The Procurement department used this balance report to adjust the purchase orders placed of raw material according to the delivery schedule.

The result was a reduction of raw material in stock.

Turning the Tide

Turning the tide

I arrived early in the morning, maybe 07:00 AM if I am not wrong, and when I saw the shop floor, I felt that incredible feeling coming from inside.

We had cleaned up the factory, the corridors were empty, the machines had a little production load or none, I felt butterflies in the spine. Would this model work? I asked to myself.

The first day was intense, Silvestre and I stayed all day long at production site floor discussing every single detail, regarding to machine set up and production flow. We ended the day without a single pump assembled.

The next day, PCP began to load the machines at production with such parts, that at the end, could create an assembly order and a product ready to be deliver.

At first hours, Nilton was not convinced of what we were doing, in his thoughts the number of set up would increase, especially at the Multidrill Head machine and the consequence would be less available hours in production, diminishing the quantity of parts produced per day.

It was necessary to think and act differently, a new mind set must be implemented at production line, then I called Nilton and Silvestre right there, near the multiple head drilling machine and questioned them about the reasons for a set up so long, and if so what we must do to reduce set up time. I offered myself to help them.

Silvestre was excited about the opportunity to adjust and upgrade the machines, because, during the old time, he only produced and made corrective maintenance. Now it was time to take a deep look into the process.

Suggestions for improvements soon appeared, it came from the machine operators and by themselves. However, it had a consequence, that was, to modify the tooling device, we had to stop the machine for a while. A question came out, for how long?

This had a price to be paid. We get into the third day with not a single unit assembled practically.

During the time spent on adjusting the machine, we manufactured parts that did not have to pass through the multiple drill head machine and these parts would go directly to the warehouse, meanwhile, the machine operators were helping the tooling and maintenance staff to speed up the service and learn a little bit more about how to get the best from this multiple head drilling machine.

The tooling personnel worked hard, they made all changes suggested by Silvestre, they took a day and a half, but at the end, we achieved our goals, we got a reduction on set up time. The job was well done.

Silvestre had bought the idea, finally.

From now on, no larger batches of parts would be produced at once, but just small batches several times. This would be the new mind set in conducting the planning and production from now on.

As a result, few units assembled on the second day after the change.

Turning the Tide

The shop floor was quiet, no noise, no stacked containers, no parts stopped in the middle of the corridors, so from anywhere in the factory we could see production´s flow.

The biggest movement was made by the tooling and maintenance staff towards the multiple head drilling machine. All others machines were running as planned.

At the end of the morning of the fourth day, the multiple head drilling machine was released by maintenance, who started its commissioning. It would produce some parts, which would be inspected and if approved, the machine would return to work.

Gerson from PCP got the news and immediately begun a planning program to complement the missing parts needed at the assembling line. We had already manufactured gears, wear plates and bodies while the multiple head drilling machine was under maintenance. We did what we planned.

It was Friday and I did not have realized how much change we had performed along the week.

We had begun a new cycle in production and in assembling lines, improved the PCP, increased the procurement, enhanced the Information Technology section to support and develop systems for the whole company. Everything appeared to have occurred in a very small fraction of time

We had started a new cycle for the whole company.

This feeling was not only mine, we could see it thru Silvestre and Nilton face and in the employee's behavior.

My belief did not change, I was sure that we could achieve the goals, we were working on to make things happen, once again I remembered my learning lessons about JUST-IN-TIME and KAN-BAN.

The fourth day had ended, and we had assembled just few units.

We closed the week with just over 80 units assembled and we had a sales forecast of 1720 units to achieve, so we had three weeks to produce and assemble 1640 units.

This would require a lot of hard work and planning.

Turning the Tide

During the weekend, my thoughts were coming up and down, the anxiety took its place, the next Monday morning did not leave my mind.

But for those who had children at age up to 5 years old, did not have much time for such feelings, the kids wanted full attention and so I did.

My wife had suggested to spend the morning at a pool in our condominium and after lunch we should go to TIJUCA Mall, a huge shopping mall that had a play center and fast food inside. This was the weekend.

I left home early in the morning every day and came back close to dinner hour, around 07:00 PM. By this time, they had already finished their dinner and were waiting for me. Be back home and be welcomed by them was priceless.

One of my wishes was a weekend house and since I got this new job at HYDRO SPECIAL, my wife and I had been thought about it, we loved to be at the lakes.

My sister-in-law had just bought a house in a condominium in the lakes region in a small town called Iguaba Grande and invited us to get together at her house for a barbecue and had some fun. We accepted the invitation.

We woke up by 06:00AM on Saturday, grappled our stuffs and put the car on the road.

On the way to Iguaba Grande, the kids started to do a great mess in the car, they asked for food, water and fought each other at the same time. Oh, My God.

We used to travel carrying sandwiches biscuits, bottles of water, diapers, snacks, all in a bag, a blue handle bag that my wife used to carry the children stuffs. The trip took a long time, because traffic jam that was common on sunny weekends.

My thoughts were on the road and on my family's safety, because the road to Iguaba Grande was hard to drive, no chance to think about the changes at the plant. It just happened when we stopped or at a traffic jam or for refueling at a gas station, so at this time everything about the changes come up to my mind.

After more than 2 hours driving, we finally arrived. I parked the car, kids drop off and gone to get together with their cousins, while my wife and I went to the backyard to help the others for preparing a barbecue.

We were back in Rio in Sunday afternoon, and as Monday was becoming closer, my thoughts over the changes prowled, Sunday has gone.

I had full conviction that we were on the right track, but I had to prove it.

I always did the same route on my way to the plant, I left home in direction to Paulo de Frontin Avenue, and then I got to Leopoldina direction and Brasil Avenue, drove for 50 minutes and finally arrived.

Turning the Tide

On that Monday, I arrived early and went straight to production line, it was around 07:40h AM, despite my labor-hours was set from 08:00h AM to 05:00h PM.

I walked directly towards Nilton, the production area was so organized, then never seen before. For those who were used to see several containers of parts spread all over the four corners, it was shocking.

Gerson from PCP was preparing a list of parts to restart the production as we had defined.

The plan was to load the machines with small lots of raw materials to be machined and sent to assembling line, where they should be assembled and tested, turning into a pump, ready to be sent to the warehouse and then invoicing.

Silvestre arrived shortly after me, maybe 15 minutes later and came to join us on the conversation about a subject that stuck all morning. What should be the lot's size?

Nilton and I were near the grinding machines and right in the middle of the shed, when Silvestre appeared. Nilton showed his point of view by arguing about the lot's size, in his opinion, the machines should be loaded at full capacity, because the time spent at set up were so high.

This certainly would be a great question. I did not know the exact answer or even approximate number to be use as lot size, we should learn from ours mistakes and lessons learn.

The fact was that I ought to manufacture, assemble and test 1640 units in three weeks, which would give me a rating of 109 units assembled and tested per day.

My proposal was a production lot of 30 pieces from each component of a pump, so at every 30 pieces manufactured we should have them routed to the assembling line and so we could measure how many units should be assembled in a day.

Edilberto, was the assembling and testing line foreman, in the past, he used to receive hundreds of parts and many of the them without its pair for assembling. He was septic about those changes, it was a matter of first seeing then believing.

The rhythm of production was still lazy, the famous Learning Curve that I heard during my graduation on Engineering at Planning and Production class was still on, but, before the end of the first shift, the first batch of 30 units reached the assembling line.

From the other side, The Board, by its turn, was supporting and was confident about the work done, but this week we ought to deliver much more than 80 units, as happened in the week before.

The organization of production was running as planned, but in other hand, other departments whose actions impacted directly on production, should be also imbued with the same spirit or involved in solving the problem.

The gears production process was divided into three stages. The first stage occurred in the rough lathe sector, where the forgings were machined.

On the second stage all gears should be sent to be heat treated in a facility outside our plant to achieve the mechanical properties and on their return, on the third stage, they should pass through a grinding machine before being released to the assembling line.

To be successful on these tasks, we were depending on contracting suppliers for services and logistics to do the job. These critical tasks were put at procurement hands, that should contract a heat treatment

Turning the Tide

supplier as so someone for transporting those gears. We were procurement department dependence.

Lemos, who was now ahead of procurement, had made a long-term contract with the company ALLTEMPER STEEL, which was about 30 km far from the factory. This company was specialized in heat treatments of ferrous materials and special steels, was set in Cordovil, whose owner, Mr. Klinger, an Austrian of some 60 years old, an expert in metallurgical engineering, whose knowledge on the subject, could help us a lot. We expected to get some tips from Klinger that could confirm the benefits from the changes done.

Before we go, I made a list of the problems to be discussed at ALLTEMPER. The first problem was about dispatching and receiving gears in a constant flow from heat treatment.

I had on my mind that, we should be looking for a heat treatment process that could fit in this new production mind set. Our problem was that the heat treatment process occurred in a not-owned facility, which means that, we had no management about it. It was a problem to solve.

The gears took about eight hours to return from ALLTEMPER, that was, if the gears were delivered by the morning, they would only return at the end of the day, impacting directly at the assembling line.

This was a real problem, because it had influenced my assembling goal, so it was necessary to find a solution. Then I called William from Supplier Development and the Quality Control chief to analyze the problem.

We must to know if there would be another technique for heat treatment, that would give us the same result in quality and should be done in a shorter time, this was a subject for Supplier Development department to solve.

I set up a meeting at ALLTEMPER to find out about Mr. Klinger technical point of view and what solution he would have and whether it would be economically feasible. We would not accept any solution that should increase our costs.

Klinger was a highly recommended metallurgist among his peers, he was not used to visitors, but in this case, which were a technical issue no problem at all, in fact what matters for him was his Metallurgy Lab, where he used to developed his studies in improvements on the heat treatment process. His daughter, Margareth was in charge with business affairs.

We were on three of us, Wiliam, Fernando and me. During the trip, I was thinking about an alternate plan, plan B, in case Klinger could not help us.

Plan B, consisted of to find a company or a supplier that could provide machining services, if possible, specialized in gears manufacturing. This would be considered as a marginal production, which in case of success, would enable us to increase our daily gear production and to achieve the assembly plan and spare parts sales, too.

This action was given to William, because of his knowledge of the market and it was part of his duty, I asked for a strategic plan for that.

Margaret was waiting for us at reception room, she took us to the lab where Klinger was. I started the meeting explaining him the ongoing changes at HYDRO SPECIAL and what were our needs and asked him if he could have a technical solution for reducing the heat treatment lead time, maintaining the actual quality patterns.

Klinger was so enthusiastic that his eyes were glowing, he gave us a school lesson about heat treatment and all the different methods to achieve the same goal. In our case, the longest time was spent on

Turning the Tide

the steel carburizing process, which was a thermochemical process, that consists of introducing atoms of carbon on the surface of a steel parts.

He gave us excellent news, ALLTEMPER could do the gas carburizing process and this would reduce the total soaking time, in a way to meet our expectations.

Margaret who also attended the meeting came up with the problem of rising costs. Our position was not to have cost increased, but I asked her to inform us how much this increase would cost and while we were discussing the new cost, the gears should be heat treated by the new method. All arranged, back to the factory.

On the way back to the plant, more than ever, the need for another source for heat treatment and one machining gear arose, these jobs were also given to Wiliam.

On the arrival, I went to the director´s room to give the good news and inform him about the tasks given to William, he took the opportunity to ask me how the changes were going. I made an explanation about what was going on and that we had planned to assemble on this Monday, at least 80 units.

I returned to my office, I called Gerson from PCP, Sidney from logistics and the warehouse foreman.

I told them about the talking that we had had with Klinger and about the transport schedule. The gears must be delivered and collected twice a day as agreed with Klinger.

So, at 08:00 AM we should transport the gears that were ready for heat treatment at the night before and return with the ones that were heat treated.

Another batch of gears to be heat treated would be dispatched at 02:00h PM to ALLTEMPER and would return with gears already heat treated in the next morning.

So, the gears needed at the assembling line was guaranteed.

It was almost 05:00PM, Monday was getting to an end and the assembling line had worked smoothly, they had already delivered 96 units to the warehouse for invoicing and still had a few in process of final assembling, great day.

Early Tuesday the board did not waited for the report that I always prepared with number of units assembled on the day before, both directors were at the assembling line talking with the foreman in charge. They wanted to know how many units were assembled and became surprised when they were told that the volume of pumps assembled on Monday was 126 units, a record in the company's history.

I met them at the assembling line and theirs doubt was if we could do it again or it was just a coincidence. Edilberto, the foreman replied that if he had more material available, he could have assembled more. So, the Board looked at me.

The ball was on my hands.

Turning the Tide

The changes in production was running as expected, slowdown in the beginning and speed up as days passed by. Every day we had lessons to learn.

The machine operators were already accepting and assimilating the new mind set, they began to feel the difference between pushing against and pulling production, the rhythm was different, it was intense, and the production flow was running much better.

The sales backlog had been monitoring by Materials Management department, not just for finished products, but also for spare parts.

Spare part was a serious problem, due to a production policy that prioritized finished products, so all orders related to spare parts were neglected, this policy were causing problems with our main customers.

The backlog was huge, so I asked Gerson from PCP to prepare a list of spare parts delayed using SIVAE software. The report showed us that, we would need more than one month of exclusive production to close all backlog. This had to change too.

The solution had to pass thru Supplier Development department. We had scheduled a meeting involving PCP, Procurement, Supplier Development and the Board. The proposal, as I had already spoken to Wiliam by the time of ALLTEMPER's visit, was to find or to develop suppliers with machining facility to produce gears. That would be our marginal production.

The strategy consisted of a development of new supplier, that could offer lathe machining services within the requirements of quality, daily production capacity and cost. This supplier must be closer to our plant for logistics reason and must have CNC lathe machines. We would supply the forgings.

We had defined some supplier´s basic characteristics for machining our forgings. The supplier must have a Quality Control System, a CNC lathe machines and daily production capacity, was the first choice.

Otherwise, in case of difficulty to find a supplier as we planned, we had another option, that was to find a company that could offer lathe rental hours, in this case, we would do the job with our machine operators.

This was a mission given to Wiliam, who with the help of quality control staff started to travel around Rio de Janeiro searching for companies to be qualified. We were all in waiting for their feedback.

The Material Management department had established a strategy involving our main suppliers, no matter what if they supplied us raw material or maintenance goods, to guarantee the supply flow, price and on time delivery, targeting a reduction of items in stock.

This strategy was based on JUST IN TIME and into the Suppliers Relationship Management philosophy, practiced through long-term contracts with minimum consumption guaranteed and adjusted periodically. This was the end of the automatic resupply policy, there would be no more order point or supply based on historical consumption and safety stock quantities, the concept for resupply using Sawtooth graphic model was abolished.

Turning the Tide

We were running towards the lowest TCO (Total Cost of Ownership).

All those changes were perceived and processed by Lemos from the Statistics. He developed a spreadsheet with cost projection for the main raw material and a monthly index that represents a relationship between raw material cost and sales price in percentage. He established an index number.

Lemos used to follow the price evolution for non-ferrous materials, especially bronze, due to wear plate costs. This component, wear plate, despite of a development of a new supplier its cost is still expensive. The new supplier brought to us a drastic reduction in problems related to foundry quality, that reflected directly on less lost labor hours on production, since then, the index of wear plate rejected parts passed to one in every ten thousand parts delivered, as per Quality Control report.

The bronze wear plates supplied by Bronze-Italy made the production manager satisfied, finally there was no loss or rejection during the milling process. The PCP could achieve its assembling target finally, and the assembling line should be fed for wear plates from production finally. This made the Procurement department happy too.

This new supplier were feeding our plant with wear plates with excellent quality, following the delivery dates and theirs price was cheaper than the previous foundry.

Lemos was the only one who ever questioned about the usage of a such expensive raw material for wear plates.

The Development of Supplier Department was created to bring solutions for raw material cost and enhance the number of suppliers for our products´ line.

So, based on that, I invited all departments that were involved in production to discuss about bronze wear plate cost.

Discussion was launched.

To understand the bronze wear plate cost composition and its influence on pump sales price, we should separate the cost into two parcels.

The first parcel was the raw material, which was expensive, and the second parcel was related to the machining process.

The rough wear plate design from Engineering specifies an extraordinary thickness that increased the milling time significantly.

In accordance with the blueprint it was necessary to machine in all three directions, spending more time, in this case, the workpiece must be 100% machined. We needed to find a way to reduce the milling time.

We discussed for hours and at the end we got into two points. One point was to ask Bronze-Italy Foundry if they could reduce the rough thickness to a minimum and the length as a finished measure and the other point was a disruptive action. The usage of aluminum instead of bronze.

We were on the morning of August 30th and the numbers of pumps assembled and delivered for invoicing pointed out to 1820 units. The Board was happy, but at the same time worried, because on the day before, in a phone call, they told to their boss in USA, that this time we would reach the milestone of 2000 units.

We still had two days more, which were the 30th and 31st of August to achieve the desired number.

The changes made and implemented in production, all adjustments in the machine devices, the reduction of the size on production lots,

Turning the Tide

the new technique for gear heat treatment and the new mind set at the Human Resources, that had made the employees spirit grew high, were responsible for this high volume of assembled and delivered units.

The average of assembled units exceeded 150 units per day, or 1970 units in theory.

Thus, on August 31st, the Board repeated the action done by the beginning of the previous month, when they argued whether we could reach 2000 units or not.

It was early in the morning and they went directly to the assembly and testing area, inquiring about how many units had been assembled. The answer came through a smile form assembling foreman, Mr Edilberto, when he confirmed that on the 31st of August, we had achieved 2096 units assembled and delivered.

It was a remarkable day, because for the first time HYDRO SPECIAL had reached the expected number.

The victory belonged to all of us.

I was on my desk in my office analyzing the production chart and preparing a detailed production report for the Board, when they entered. They thanked me for the dedication, congratulated for the result, but asked how September would be.

The message left by this question gave an idea of a certain doubt about all we had done. This demonstrated how suspicious the Board were. I still had to prove that we were on the right track.

I thought to myself, would it have been a coincidence or competence?

This should be answered on the next month.

Vinicius Rabello de Abreu Lima

Turning the Tide

September begun and the production and assembling line were running smoothly. The production philosophy continued to be "pulling instead of pushing" the production flow, but we still had a long way to go, in terms of a stable production flow, sales orders delivered and to satisfy our customers.

Things had changed since then, but we were still facing some difficulties. We were waiting for a budget approval to update our lathe machine line into an automated one.

The bronze wear plates cost was still high, the new gear hob tool and the new personal computers had not arrived yet and we were still not supplying pump´s spare parts to our customers. Problems we had and a lot.

The new Material Management department established a follow up routine for every development requested with an engagement of purchasing, quality control and engineering personnel.

For the first action, we decided to put all our efforts on a development program for manufacturing gears outside HYDRO SPECIAL facilities.

This action was given to William from Supplier Development department.

Wiliam together with an inspector from Quality Control had visited so many companies, but none of them had met a minimum qualification status required. Rio de Janeiro had insufficient machining service providers for that purpose.

During his trip along Rio de Janeiro, William discovered in Nilopolis a company called SOARES Mechanical Center, which had recently made a technical agreement with the Italian government and bought new CNC lathes machines from Italian companies.

He was quite sure that this company could be a solution provider for manufacturing gears.

Since then, PCP was working online with production, purchasing and sales, using SIVAE, a system developed by Nakayama for MRP, allowing PCP personnel to have a long-term view about the planning.

SIVAE gave to PCP personnel, an exploded view for every model on sales forecast, listing everything needed to be bought and produced, considering all parts that were already in production or ready in stock.

The production inventory was the input for updating the assembling products list. The SIVAE system created a table of missing parts that should be updated from production inventory, after that, SIVAE issued several assembly services orders to attempt a sale's forecast or a confirmed sales order.

Time had passed and Silvestre could not update his lathes, the budget was not approved by the Board, but he made a great effort to convince the Industrial Director to agree in buying a new titanium-coated gear hob to opening the gears' tooth. This new gear hob too would increase in 40% the quantity of machined parts.

We were now depended on supplier development to increase gear production, through a marginal production at the SOARES Mechanical Center, if they were approved by our Quality Control and

Turning the Tide

their cost was in our budget, we could finally comply with the delivery of spares gears.

At the assembly line we had already performed 1300 units assembled and delivered by the beginning of the third week of September, the revenues increased and for the second month, we were producing without overjumps, much of this was due to the preventive maintenance plan for the milling machines. The machine operators were less stressed.

Purchases closed a contract with SOARES Mechanical Center, after receiving the company qualification report issued by William from the Supplier Development department and sharing this the information with Gerson from PCP and Nilton from Production, so they prepared an extraordinary gear production program to SOARES. We would supply the forgings and lathe operator.

Now we had two lines for producing gears, increasing the logistics complexity from carrying and bringing gears between the two facilities, and the management of the displacement of 2 lathe operators, but the results expected were enormous.

The procurement department and its policy of establishing strategic partnerships with the main suppliers, could reduce the total costs of ownership of raw materials, maintaining the specified quality patterns and deliveries on time in the expected volume, resulting in a short inventory.

September had reached an end, we had solved one big problem, that was how to increase gear production.

The production line was flowing as expected, the procurement department kept the factory stocked and the assembling line fed, which led us to reach 2210 units by the end of September.

We really were on the right track.

In the remaining months until the end of the year, an average of 2100 units per month were assembled and delivered, turning to null the sales´ backlog, including the spare parts.

The pressure was now at Sales department.

Turning the Tide

End of November, we were almost entering December, the Board had just returned from the annual meeting with the CEO at the headquarters, where they presented the annual result of HYDRO SPECIAL.

According to them, our peers at the major company were interested about the change made in Brazil, they wanted to know a little bit about the whole process, specially the usage of Personnel Computers in a MRP program, because they had spent a lot of money in a computerized system on an IBM4340.

HYDRO SPECIAL would start a new year with a materials management that could successfully deploy a Supplier Relationship Management system, adopt a JUST IN TIME philosophy for strategic and critical components, reduce the cost of raw materials acquisition with a consequent reduction of total cost of ownership (TCO).

The change occurred in planning and production thru the adoption of KANBAN philosophy, focusing in pulling and not pushing the production together with KAIZEN philosophy of continuous improvement process, helped the company to understand the market behavior and made our customers satisfied, so these led us to achieve our goals and pleased the major company CEO.

The support from the Board of directors in Brazil was of fundamental importance for the Supplier Development department, which contributed significantly to cost reduction, by the development new suppliers, but especially by the technological solutions, they had brought.

The gear's heat treatment solution provided by ALLTEMPER was an example of the State-of-the-Art available in the market and incorporated into our process, as so the usage of aluminum wear plates and Titanium coated gear hob, in addition to other actions of enormous importance to HYDRO SPECIAL.

The usage of Personal Computers into our routines was not a small dream, but a great reality, through the dissemination of microcomputers by all departments, we could have more accuracy about the data processed, assisting the decision-making process.

During this period, errors made, doubts and questions arose, which had made us think about to be more conservative and not change so much, but never give up or fade in what we believed.

At the end of the changing process, the satisfaction of those who had worked hard, faced and won the challenges was incommensurable.

A new year begun, HYDRO SPECIAL was now at another level, and prepared to attempt the market needs.

HYDRO SPECIAL had overcome the challenges.

Annex 1 – Porter´s 5 Forces

Michael E Porter created a model that identifies and analyzes five competitive forces that shape every industry. These five forces help to determine an industry's weaknesses and strengths.

We can use to identify an industry's structure to determine corporate strategy.

HYDRO SPECIAL Market Analysis for castings

Porter´s 5 Forces are

1. Competition in the industry;
2. Potential of new entrants into the industry;
3. Power of customers;
4. Power of suppliers;
5. Threat of substitute products.

Evaluation	Score
VERY HIGH	5
High	4
Average	3
Low	2
VERY LOW	1
ZERO	0

i. Competition in the industry

Subjects	Classification	Points
Number of direct competitors	Very High	5
Market power of direct competitors	Average	3
Market loss for competitors	Average	3
What make your company different?	High	4
Production Costs/service delivery	High	4
Price of your product/service	Average	3
How easy you can adapt to changes	Low	2

Turning the Tide

ii. Potential of new entrants into the industry

Subjects	Classification	Points
Number of new companies entering into the same market as yours	Very High	5
Loss of your market share for new entrants	Very low	1
How government policies affect your company	Low	2
Existence of strategies to reduce the impacts of new incoming threats	Very Low	1
What these companies had as a differential from yours?	High	5

iii Power of customers

Subjects	Classification	Points
Impact of the Purchaser's customer-given value on the potential of its client/supplier	Average	3
Significant portion of the supplier's total turnover is derived from a few customers	Low	2
Degree of negotiation power of these few customers	Low	2
Existence of strategies to mitigate the effects of trading power of these clients	Low	2
What does your customers know about the market	Very High	5
How important your products/services are to customers	High	4

Turning the Tide

iv Power of Suppliers.

Subjects	Classification	Points
Reliance on your company with one or more vendors	VERY HIGH	5
Possibility of replacing suppliers ' products	Average	3
Degree of importance of your company to suppliers	Average	3
Existence of strategies to mitigate the effects of dependence on suppliers	Average	3
Costs involved in changing vendor	VERY LOW	1
Degree of demand from suppliers of your company	VERY LOW	1

v.   Threat of substitute products.

Subjects	Classification	Points
Existence of the possibility of product or service can perform the same function that your company carries out.	Average	3
Loss of sales due to substitute products.	Average	3
Existence of strategies implemented to compete with these products/services.	Very Low	1
Degree of development of products/services by your company different from those already existing.	Average	3
Chances of these new substitute products/services change your customers ' preferences.	Average	3

Turning the Tide

Calculation of the average of each item having as reference the sum of points divided by the number of questions raised in each item.

Description	Issues	Sum	Average
Competition in the industry	7	24	3,49
New Entrants	5	14	2,80
Power Buyer	6	18	3,00
Power Supplier	6	16	2,67
Substitute Products	5	13	2,60

Representative graph of the five Porter forces for cast iron parts for HYDRO SPECIAL

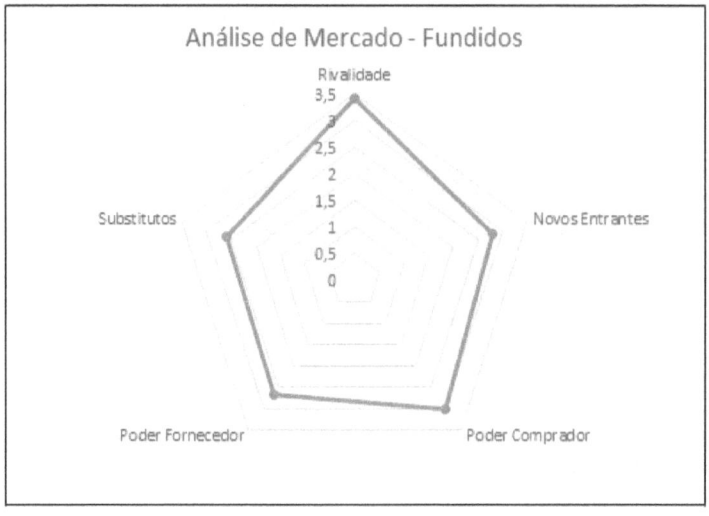

Figure 10-Porter force for cast parts

www.ingramcontent.com/pod-product-compliance
Lightning Source LLC
Chambersburg PA
CBHW021450210526
45463CB00002B/716